Color Photo Guide

# Rhine

## MIDDLE RHINE FROM MAINZ TO COLOGNE

**rahmel**verlag®
deutschlandkultur. entdecken!

# Index

# The Rhine between Mainz and Cologne

Western Europe's mightiest river carries the most traffic in the world and is a child of the mountains. There are mountain ranges within sight of its banks all the way to Bonn. They keep their distance from one another between Basel and Mainz, but when they reach the Rheingau region they become close once more. From Bingen, the Rhine valley becomes a gorge. The river forces itself through the narrow pass for 60 kilometres to Coblenz. The splendid Lorely narrows it to a total 90-metre width and its current becomes rapid. The walls of this gorge are steep, and jagged and ribbed in places. Some slopes are wooded, whilst others only have sparse undergrowth and where the sun has got through there are steep terraces planted with vines. The winemakers must have a good head for heights here, as they go about their work high above the riverbed, often on only a couple of feet of steep ground. There are glorious vineyards at Rüdesheim, Aßmannshausen, Bingen, Bacharach, Boppard and further downstream also at Unkel, Königswinter and other places. The height of the cliffs on both sides is easily underestimated. The riverbed at Mainz is 80 metres above sea level, 65 at Coblenz and the mountains reach 500 metres throughout. Thus, the Middle Rhine gorge is a good 400 metres deep. It is not just nature that has influenced the grandest part of the Rhine Valley. A lot of its charms are man-made. Franconian villages grew together out of fishing huts along the banks, often protected by fortified aristocratic seats. Thus, craftsmen and traders settled together. The toll collection points of the Rhine princes did not make the local citizens poor, as the little people also benefited from the profits of the great. The Knights of Hunsrück and Taunus built true palaces on the steep faces. You will not find castles so close together anywhere else in the world. In 1689, when French King Louis XIV seized the most fertile source of money in Europe, the "Rhine duties" (Rheinzölle), he had these witnesses to German history burnt to the ground. Only three of the many proud castles survived: the Marksburg, the Rheinfels and the Ehrenbreitstein. The latter was demolished by the locals in 1801, five years after the Rheinfels. Behind Coblenz, the river settles comfortably in its bed once more and swells to a mighty width. It flows by the castle-topped peaks of the Siebengebirge mountains, past Bonn and through the Rhine metropolis of Cologne towards the lowlands. The Prussians arrived in 1815. Their motto was regeneration of the "old German architecture". They restored many of the ruined castles in the upper Middle Rhine region, which was declared a World Heritage Site by UNESCO in 2002. This unique landscape matches the cheerful nature of its inhabitants, which still finds its most famous expression in the Rhine Carnival in the strongholds of Mainz and Cologne.

# Mainz

For over 2,000 years now, Mainz, from across the Rhine, has controlled the mouth of the Main tributary. It was under the name "Moguntiacum" that the Romans, in 38 B.C., combined a few Celtic villages to form the fortified **capital of Germania Superior**. Extensive remains of the Roman water conduits can be seen on the western outskirts of the city. About 300 A. D., Mainz became an episcopal seat. During the age of the great migrations, Mainz underwent regular destruction. In 745, Boniface, missionary to the Franks, chose the city as centre for the fist archbishopric on German soil. His subordinates were bishops far to the west, past Aschaffenburg and beyond Halle, Erfurt and Eichsfeld. The great **Cathedral of Mainz** was founded by Archbishop Willigis (975 – 1011). Centuries have embellished, enlarged, enriched it. Seven coronations took place within its walls. The oldest section of the structure is the massive eastern choir and the lower levels of the stair turrets accompanying it. The main building, dating from the 12th century, has three naves and is separated from the elevated choir by a transept. The intersection of the two is covered by a domical vault. Over this rises the eastern crossing tower, lower today than that over the western crossing. Huge round pillars separate the main nave from the narrower and lower side aisles. All three divisions have cross vaulting and are modestly lit by Romanesque windows. More light and spare are suggested by the **west choir** area. It, too, is fronted by a transept, extending much farther than the one in the east. The opulent features betray its origin in the late Hohenstaufen period. In fact, the two basements of the **western crossing tower** were not completed until 1239, the high Gothic glass house on top as far as the clock gallery in 1490, and the showy, but elegant crowning element only added in 1767 – 74, following a fire, by Michael Neumann, son of the brilliant Balthasar Neumann. The rich interior of the west choir, too, is a product of the 18th century. On the market side of the Cathedral is the double chapel of St. Gotthart, a room full of dignity, dedicated in 1137. 109 metres is the full measure of the Cathedral's length. The **tombs of the city's archbishops**, 13th to 18th centuries, adorn the pillars and inner walls, a medieval pageantry of Death Triumphant. Many are magnificent examples of the stonemason's art. The Cathedral's two choir areas are reached by flights of broad stairs. Below are the two crypts. On the market side, the Cathedral is structurally united with shops, marking the day-to-day contact with the life of the city. Nestling against the longitudinal front in the south is the noble and serene medieval cloister. One of the four wings has a display of remains of old structural sculpture, including fragments of the splendid west rood screen showing the Last Judgement. Dated pre 1239, this is deemed to be a fine specimen of the world-famous Naumburger Master's art. The 1766 fire, caused by lightning, in the west of the Cathedral dam-

Cathedral of Mainz ▷

aged this masterpiece of medieval sculpture so severely that it had to be taken down. Even under the Ottonians, the Archbishops of Mainz were already archchancellors of the Empire. After 1257, they chaired the seven-member electoral college responsible for choosing German kings. **"Golden Mainz"** emerged, with rich burghers' quarters, nobles' residences, parish church and church of its order, in the centre of medieval Germany. Emperor Frederick Barbarossa held his Imperial Diet here. The city was fortified, and its business boomed. Intellectual life, too, flourished. City son **Johannes Gutenberg** invented **printing** from movable type around 1440. The **University** was founded in 1477, existed till 1798, and was reopened in 1946. The havoc caused by the Thirty Years' War, 1631, again in 1793 and 1945, was invariably remedied at once. Of the rich heritage of historic structures, what has survived, in addition to the Cathedral and the even older **Johanniskirche**, includes Gothic buildings like the churches of **St. Quintin**, 13th – 15th century, and **St. Stephan**, with its prominent tower. The **Electoral Palace**, a fine Renaissance structure, now houses the **Central Roman-Germanic Museum** with its unique treasures. The coloured **Market Fountain** is one more Renaissance masterpiece. Magnificent **Baroque churches** (St. Peter, St. Ignaz, 1763 – 74, Augustinerkirche) and **Rococo stately homes**, like the Osteiner Hof, Bassenheimer Hof, Schönborner Hof, now hosting the Institut Français, Erthaler Hof, Dalberger Hof, still set the tone in Mainz. The **Arsenal** (Zeughaus) and many other buildings help produce the sophistication of the present-day **capital of the State of Rhineland-Palatinate**. To the connoisseur, this is a paradise for wine, asparagus and other epicurean delights, but offering more down-to-earth hospitality as well. Mainz's Carnival, called "Fasenacht", is world-famous and attracts innumerable visitors every year. The musical genius of a highly gifted tribe combines with jest, satire, irony and a splash of profundity to create an unprecedented brilliance. **Passenger shipping** down the Rhine starts at Mainz. This is the home, too, of the nation-wide **TV network ZDF**, and of the **World Printing Museum**, located in Gutenberg's workshop, restored with true high fidelity. "Mainz bleibt Mainz", they say: Mainz will be Mainz.

△ Mainz

Cathedral of Mainz, Renaissance-Fountain ▽

## Wiesbaden

Of Wiesbaden's Roman childhood little has survived. There is evidence that the hot springs there were being used in the 1st century A. D. In 112 A. D., the successor to Roman castra was calledn "Aquae Mattiacorum". 370 saw a protective wall built round springs and settlement. Against Germanic tribes? In 829, we come across the name "Wisibada", employed by the chronicler Einhard to refer to the local royal court. After 1250, the town passed to the counts of Nassau. Their lion adorns the **Market Fountain**, 1537, in front of the old **Town Hall**, 1609, used today as registry office. The House of Nassau gave the town residence status. At the Rhine, in **Wiesbaden-Biebrich**, they built the delightful **Rococo palace**, 1744. As late as 1837 – 41, they erected a town house in the Classic Revival style right in the heart of Wiesbaden. It now houses the Hessian state parliament. In 1866, Nassau, like Hesse-Kassel, was annexed by the Prussians. The new masters developed the town into one of Germany's chief spas. Cultural life received a boost. The **Staatstheater** came to be one of the leading German theatres. The **casino** in the elegant city on the southern slopes of the Taunus mountains attracts paying guests from all over the world. The streetscape was modernized on the Berlin pattern. The features of the Colonial style given to all of Prussia's new acquisitions after 1866 survived World War II only in Wiesbaden. Even today, the city presents a rare insight into the design philosophy of those expansionary "Gründerjahre": wide boulevards with hotels and business houses behind façades that vie with the Baroque. Only after the Staatstheater and the colonnades of its environs was a **casino of a health resort** (Kurhaus) in the latest style built in 1907 for the **Kochbrunnen**, Wiesbaden's immensely rich medicinal spring. Ever since the birth of the Federal Republic, Wies-

On the Neroberg: Nero Tempel

Greek Chapel

Kurhaus

baden has been capital of the State of Hesse. A dense communications network links the city with Frankfurt and nearby Mainz. Competition with two such self-willed neighbours is something Hesse's seat of government has to live with. And it copes, which is to its credit, proving it has a power of its own. The city's importance is due to its situation, its warm climate, the hot springs and its Southern-style expansiveness. Exemplary new spa facilities have been created in the Aukammtal. Latter-day sights in Wiesbaden include the proud neo-Gothic **Market Church**, and the **Greek Chapel** on the Neroberg hill with its golden cupolas and the fine view of the Rheingau. The way up is by water-powered mountain railway. Yet, it is not such details that account for the charm of Hesse's state capital. It is the overall effect that counts. It's something in the air. Wiesbaden is the grande dame among Germany's capitals.

## Eltville

The wine from the oldest township in the Rheingau is one delectable reason for visiting this famous wine-growing area. It was being made here by the archbishops of Mainz at a very early date. To this end, they needed roomy cellars and the protection of a castle, where they could take their ease. And often did. When the Swedes advanced on Mainz in 1632, they blew up the hall building of the Eltvillian **Electoral Castle** in passing. Yet, they were no match for the mighty castle tower, which now houses the **Gutenberg Museum**. Remains of the town's fortifications, stately houses redolent of old wine, and the **town church** with its Gothic murals and figures make Eltville a must for art-lovers.

Electoral Castle

## Monastery Eberbach

This most important medieval sacred building in the Rheingau was started in 1135 by the Cistercians. It was their second establishment on German soil. The emissaries of Bernard of Clairvaux, the order's founder, sought out, as always, a quiet wooded valley, and completed church and monastery before the 12th century was out. The big estate has largely retained its medieval structures, and is looked after by the State of Hesse, for the **Wine Academy** is here. The huge vaulted refectory and dormitory of the monastery's former dwellers are each bigger than the beautiful, nearly 80-metre-long church. The splendid stellar vault of the **chapter house** rests on one single central support.

# Oestrich

The **Mittelheim** district of Oestrich boasts the oldest surviving Romanesque church in the Rheingau: the St. Ägidius basilica, 12th cent. **St. Martin's** in Oestrich may be older, but was renewed in 1509. The core of the **Town Hall**, too, was built soon after 1500. The old **Rhine Crane** has machinery going back to 1652 that is still fully intact. Local festive occasions are the **Dippemarkt** and its **Lenchenfest**. "Lenchen" is the pride and joy of this largest wine-growing town in the Rheingau, a hillside of widely extolled wine. Oestrich is rich in old **burgher's houses** from late Gothic to Rococo. Germany's oldest stone building is located in the **Winkel** district: das **Graue Haus**.

Oestrich, Old Rhine Crane (1652)

Ingelheim, Parish Church (1200), Town Wall

# Ingelheim

About 800 A. D., Charlemagne built his favorite Imperial court at Ingelheim, half-way between Mainz and Bingen behind the left bank of the Rhine. Its great throne room, the royal hall, also known as the "Reichssaal", was the handsomest secular building in Germany's early Middle Ages. In 1689, it was destroyed by the French, who only left the scanty remains still visible today. 1,200-year-old Ingelheim owes its present prosperity to red wine and asparagus. It also has Europe's oldest cherry market. Town son **Sebastian Münster** was author of the "Baseler Cosmographei", 1544, the chief cosmography of that century.

# Rüdesheim

The Rhine has majestically traversed the sunny Rheingau, westward bound. Not even the tree-crowned river isles could hold things up. But now there is a mountain wall in the way, offering resistance, checking its course, with pressure coming from the Hunsrück on the left and the Niederwald on the right, where the vine has ousted the trees from the slopes. The Hunsrück hills opposite are less amiable, inexorably forcing the Rhine to wheel to the north. The change of scene is sudden. Just now, the river was wallowing in expansive abundance, the waves reflecting the town of Rüdesheim. But here, hard-pressed by its own momentum, it enters a hole called the Binger Loch, at a point where a shelf of rock lies athwart the river bend, overgrown with the Mäuseturm island. The water gurgles, bubbles and foams its way over the jagged rocks into the defile. Here, reinforcements arrive from the left in the shape of the Nahe tributary to step up the pressure in this area, where the Rhine is held captive by the hills. Rüdesheim is rightly the Mecca of all pilgrims to today's Middle Rhine. It has its back to the warm south wall that fronts the Taunus mountains but is only half as high. Which explains the wall's name: Low Wood (Niederwald). Its sunny location is God's gift to wine. Yet, Rüdesheim owes just as much to the river. The rocks in the river bed of the Binger Loch made the Rhine virtually unnavigable at this dangerous spot in the old days. It was not until some 150 years ago that a permanent serviceable channel was blasted through the rock. Previously, the boatmen had invariably discharged their cargo at Rüdesheim to cart it as far as Lorch, from which point shipping was again regarded as safe. And Rüdesheim had profited from this transhipment from time immemorial. So, the town's

Rüdesheim, Rhine Panorama

12

Thrush Street △

prosperity had always had two sources: the Rhine and the wine. The town now lives from tourism. And tourists come for the wine. That polished, inviting, infectious joie de vivre which was always at home in Rüdesheim is spontaneous, casting its spell on every visitor. Half-forgotten memories of old legends surrounding local castles and old families lend wings to the imagination, populating the evening hours with fine ladies in long robes and dignified merchants with fat purses and worried brows. In the Thrush Street (**Drosselgasse**) lane, all of this is laced with more down-to-earth delights from kitchen and cellar to produce some rollicking high spirits. Wine growers have no trouble selling their wine here, although the landlords may have trouble getting more supplies. The influx of visitors, particularly at weekends, assumes proportions that local production cannot always cope with. Wine consumption at Rüdesheim alone provides a living for all the wine growing towns along the Middle Rhine. There's no end of sights here. Rhine shipping itself is an unequalled spectacle. On the river bank, one of the town's three castles has survived in all its glory: **Brömserburg Castle**, now a wine museum. This is where Mainz's Electors, too, used to hold wine-tasting sessions. And Goethe, favorite son of nearby Frankfurt, was here, according to the visitors' book, back in 1814. Yet, the noble

Adlerturm                                                In the Thrush Street

14

Cable railway to the Niederwald Monument

family of the Brömsers of Rüdesheim had died out in 1668. Then, there are other **stately houses** like that of the Bassenheimer, the Ritter of Grün, the Brömsers from the collateral line related by marriage to the Greiffenclaus at Vollrads Castle, or the Sickinger Hof, which once belonged to the family of the renowned Franz of Sickingen. The 14th century **Catholic parish church**, too, is worth a visit. The wounds left by the severe bombing of World War II have long since healed. The weathervane with its star and crescent moon recall the Turkish wars. Among other survivals is part of the town's fortifications: the late Gothic **Adlerturm**. Rüdesheim has one more speciality to offer. Something quite unique, in fact, and a must for music-lovers: **Siegfried's Mecha-**

Brömserburg Castle

**nisches Musikkabinett**, which has found a home in the Brömserhof. That collector gathered together 250 automatic music reproducers from the 150 years prior to 1930, a veritable treasure-house of inventions. Mechanical music was a forerunner of gramophone record, tape and radio. Such instruments were being designed all of 1,500 years ago in Byzantium. And there was a regular cult in the 18th and 19th centuries. In Rüdesheim, the specimens on show are virtually perfect. A comparison with modern phono equipment is well worth while.

Rüdesheim, Rhine Street

# Niederwald Monument

High above the Rhine Valley, where Rüdesheim's vineyards come up against the tree line of the Niederwald, stands the huge iron image of Germania. This symbol of Germany's regained unity was erected, 1877 – 83, and paid for by donations from the whole nation. The figure alone measures 10.55 metres from top to toe. Its 25 metres high socle is adorned with a triumphal bronze relief showing men of all branches of the armed forces, along with Emperor William I and German princes, commanders and the founder of the new Empire, Bismarck: 200 life-size figures in all. The relief is flanked by the winged female giants representing war and peace. Figures on such a scale have a history. Going back to the stone colossi of Easter Island, or to soon after 1400 B. C., when Pharaoh Amenophis III had two giant figures erected in Egyptian Thebes. About 450 B. C., Phidias the Greek produced a 10 metres high bronze figure of Athena Parthenos, which stood for over 700 years on the Acropolis of Athens. In 285 B. C., the 32 metres high bronze statue of Helios-Apollo was placed astride of the entrance to the harbour of Rhodes and became one of the Seven Wonders of the World. The late Middle Ages saw a revival of "Big is Beautiful" all over Europe. In 1404, Bremen set up a great stone Roland in front of the City Hall. Soon after, the huge Christophorus in Cologne Cathedral was completed. Both found imitators in half Europe. Giants in bronze were to come back into fashion much later. Above Wilhelmshöhe Castle at Kassel stands the mighty Hercules, built just before 1800, while work started in 1838 on the 26 metres high figure of Cheruscan leader Arminius for the western slope of the Teutoburg Forest. One more giant figure of world stature is the 46-metre-high Statue of Liberty, French gift to the United States for the approaches to New York. So, the Germania up on the Niederwald really is in a tradition – a big one, in fact. From here, you can gaze over Rüdesheim's wine-grown slopes

▽ Bronze relief „Die Wacht am Rhein"     Niederwald Monument near Rüdesheim ▷

into the staggering expanses of the Rheingau and the intimacy of the lower Nahe valley. It would be hard to find more captivating landscape opposites. The Niederwald summit can be reached by cableway from both Assmannshausen and Rüdesheim.

Niederwald Monument near Rüdesheim

# Bingen

In Roman times, a citadel on the site of the later castle controlled the intersection of the roads to Mainz, Koblenz, Trier and Kreuznach, as well as the Roman Nahe bridge. Rome's Frankish heirs made royal property of the Roman structures, and that was handed over by Emperor Otto II to the archbishops of Mainz. The new possessions were guarded by Klopp Castle built on the Roman foundation walls, and the town fortified with walls and towers. Still, Bingen was totally destroyed three times, so the inventory of historic buildings is modest. No burgher's house is older than 1689. All fortified structures were removed in the 19th century. Just the same, the town is neat, hospitable

Bingen, Mouth of Nahe

and lively. Since 1977 it has had a quiet pedestrian zone. The Catholic parish church of **St. Martin's** was collegiate church in 1006. The Early Romanesque basilica burned down in 1403, but a new structure was completed in 1416. In 1502 – 05, the Late Gothic Barbara building with its two aisles was added as parish church to the middle nave on the left. The severe damage inflicted by World War II was finally healed in 1958. The Early Romanesque crypt betrays a debt to Speyer. The church is well-endowed with good sculpture. The side altars in the middle nave boast fine clay figures of St. Barbara and St. Catherine, dated about 1425. **Klopp Castle**, blown up in 1711 by troops from Mainz, so that

Bingen, Rochus Chapel (1666)

no foe could get established there, was rebuilt, 1875 – 1879. Today, it serves as town hall and local history museum. The **Drusus Bridge** over the Nahe, Germany's oldest bridge in the Middle Ages, was widened and renewed, 1951 – 52, after war damage. The splendidly situated **Rochus Chapel** on an elevation south of Bingen was erected after the plague year, 1666, destroyed in 1795 and rebuilt in 1814, after which it was visited by Goethe. Struck by lightning in 1889, the building burned out. Its unique location and newly acquired works of art from olden times make the new structure, consecrated in 1895, but in the old style, into an architectural work of a high standard.

Bingen, Klopp Castle

## The Mäuseturm – Legend and Reality

Below the mouth of the Nahe, an island has struck root in the bed of the Rhine. It carries a slender tower built, legend has it, by an Archbishop of Mainz called Hatto to fleece Rhine bargees. Peasants were levied the corn tithe, which he collected in a huge barn at Mainz. Following a bad harvest, the hungry rural population came to Mainz and asked for grain. This Hatto promised the petitioners, whom he sent to the tithe barn. Here he had them locked up, and he is said to have set fire

Bingen, Mice Tower (13th century)

personally to the wooden structure. All of the captives perished. Only the mice escaped. They invaded the palace and gobbled up everything edible. Then, Hatto recalled the tower on the Rhine islet, where he hoped he would be safe from the rodents. But when he reached Bingen to be ferried across, the mice were waiting for him. They swam after the boat, and many reached the tower, where they attacked Hatto and ate him alive. In fact, this "Mice Tower" (Mäuseturm) was for centuries the "Toll Tower" (Mautturm) of the Electors of Mainz, and popular imagination did the rest. It was burnt down by the French in 1689, but restored by the King of Prussia in 1855 to be used as a signal tower for the narrow shipping passage, a function the structure retained until 1974, when the channel was again deepened. Since then, the Mäuseturm has been inhabited by bats and legends.

## Ehrenfels Castle Ruin

Located down-river from Rüdesheim, twin-towered Ehrenfels Castle, from the impregnable elevation of the vineyards on the left bank, controls the exit of the Binger Loch. The lords of Bolanden, two brothers in the service of the Electors of Mainz and specialists in building castles, erected the sophisticated customs station about 1211. After 1356, the castle was extended to make a fortified court for the Electoral Archbishops, who spent war-times there. It withstood several sieges in the

Ehrenfels Castle Ruin (around 1211)

Thirty Years' War, but not the efforts of French experts in burning down castles, 1689. Much of the masonry has survived as a picturesque ruin. On the side facing the hill, the structure was protected by a 4.5-metre thick curtain wall connecting the two strong corner towers. Of other buildings only the outer walls are still to be seen. At the foot of Ehrenfels, there was once a house for the customs officials and a storage hall by the river. The brilliantly designed installations once included the Mäuseturm, wrapt in its legends on its Rhine island.

Assmannshausen, Rhine Panorama

## Assmannshausen

To the lover of fine red wines, the very name has a flavour. The clay slate slopes down to the Rhine are the birthplace of a choice late Burgundy (Spätburgunder). For nearly 200 years, Assmannshausen's **"Höllenberg"** has been attracting illustrious wine connoisseurs in flocks to the Rhine. Elegant accommodation was built at the turn of the century. All the beautiful half-timbered houses in the narrow lanes of the town centre were overshadowed by the stately inns along the river. Yet, the town has a lot of nostalgia to offer. "Hasemanneshusen" is first mentioned in a document dated 1108. Even after 1300, Assmannshausen still belonged to Rüdesheim, as it now does again, but it has a character of its own. The **Church**, built in its present form prior to 1500 on the site of an older structure, has painted altars, 15th and 18th centuries, and a fine Madonna, pre-1500. Assmannshausen is highly recommended as gateway to the wooded hills of the Taunus. There is a chairlift here for a comfortable ride to the Niederwald monument. Walkers are rewarded with some interesting views of the indented Rhine Valley.

Assmannshausen, Rhine-bank-street

## Rheinstein Castle

The castle above Trechtingshausen is said to have been first mentioned in documents around 1300. In its walls, King Rudolph of Habsburg passed unethical death sentences in 1282 on nobly born highwaymen from the neighbouring castles of Reichenstein and Sooneck. They were hanged, but there is no report of their being exposed to wind and

Rheinstein Castle

weather in the "penalty box" up on the keep. At any rate, that iron cage became the symbol of justice on the Rhine. In 1323, the Electorate of Mainz made the building into a bulwark against the Counts Palatine. Entrusted to a steward (Vogt), it was now called "Vogtsburg". These stewards included a number of noted personalities. After 1572, the old structure fell into decay, and was a ruin when the Swedes arrived in 1632. The reconstruction starting in 1825 and the name Rheinstein were due to Prince Frederick William of Prussia. He had the premises opulently painted and furnished. The present owner, Hermann Hecher, has had castle and chapel renovated, provided access to the crypt and opened this fine castle to the public. Rheinstein is a gem of romantic medievalism.

# Reichenstein Castle

From of old, the Reichenstein property had belonged to the distant Abbey of Kornelimünster near Aachen. The castle is said to have been built in the 11th century and is one of the oldest on the Rhine, being first mentioned in 1214. The robber barons having been dislodged, the honorable lords of Bolanden, who built Ehrenfels, now became stewards in Reichenstein. On behalf of Mainz, presumably, but with no lasting effect as yet. The next castellans reverted to highway robbery. In 1253, the League of Rhine Cities had to destroy Reichenstein but, in 1282, King Rudolph of Habsburg again had to evict the robbers from their lair and burn it down. Not until 1323, when the Electorate of Mainz purchased the castle site, was it possible to renew the fortified structure. Like Ehrenfels, this new, Gothic building had a mighty wall of masonry between its two flanking towers, 8 metres thick at the bottom, 5 at the top, and 16 metres high. Yet, it could not prevent the castle falling into decay. In 1899, the ruin passed into private hands. The castle was rebuilt, and now has a respectable art collection, together with a hotel and tavern. The town of Trechtingshausen at its feet has remains of the its old fortifications. Its most important structure is the Klemens Chapel, located on the upstream side, a late Romanesque masterpiece with old murals and late Gothic choir stalls.

Reichenstein Castle (11th century)

## Sooneck Castle

The property of the rich Abbey of Kornelimünster once extended to the impregnable Sooneck Castle on the Middle Rhine. Fortified with walls and battlements, it is perched high above the Rhine Valley, below Reichenstein. Stewards in both castles feathered their noble nests in the Emperorless years after 1254. In 1273, however, Rudolph of Habsburg was elected King. He hated robbers, even the aristocratic variety. In 1282, he starved the Sooneckers into submission, stringing them up, to the dismay of their kindred and brothers in arms, on the oaks round the Klemens Chapel of Trechtingshausen. Sooneck Castle was burned down and reconstruction forbidden. Not until 1323 did the Counts Palatinate of the Rhine dare ignore the ban. That was when the Electorate of Mainz acted and seized the half-finished structure. The marshals of Waldeck now managed Sooneck Castle as vassals of the Electors till their family became extinct in 1444. 200 years later, the castle was deserted. The Waldeck heirs, too, had died out. In 1689, the French blew up the empty shell. In 1843, Prussia's King Frederick William IV had Sooneck rebuilt. Fine furniture, 200 years old, Rhine views and weapons galore, not to mention the Old German tavern, all await visitors to this proud castle.

Sooneck Castle (11th century)

Heimburg Castle above Niederheimbach

## Heimburg Castle

The Wittelsbachers had had a base on the Rhine since 1214. In the office of Count Palatine, they made sure of the residence belonging to it: Stahleck Castle above Bacharach. From here, they tried to establish links with their possessions in Southern Germany. Such moves were resisted by the Electors of Mainz, good chessplayers that they were, who placed a castle in the Bavarians' way as from 1290: the Heimburg. Completed in 1305, it was located just above Niederheimbach, the border town between the archbishoprics of Mainz and Trier, although the town itself belonged to the Abbey of Kornelimünster. Under the latter's stewards, it was hard to tell the cops from the robbers along the Middle Rhine, so the whole rather troublesome property was sold to the Electorate of Mainz in 1270. Heimburg Castle lost all its value on the chessboard when Reichenstein finally passed to Mainz in 1344. Although refortified in 1475, it soon fell into decay. The French blew up what was left in 1689. Some 90 years ago, industrial magnate Hugo Stinnes rendered it habitable again and lived in the shade of its two unequal towers. It has remained private property, and is not open to the public.

## Fürstenberg Ruin

Cologne's archbishop Engelbert I had Fürstenberg Castle erected above the township of Rheindiebach in 1219, ostensibly to protect Cologne's property around Bacharach. The real reason had to do with the Rhine tolls he proposed to collect here, rather far upstream from Cologne and much too close to the customs posts of Mainz's archbishops and those of the Counts Palatine. As from 1214, the latter were the Wittelsbachs from Bavaria, who now had to dislodge the Colonians from Fürstenberg. The castle's builder died suddenly in 1225 and the structure was acquired soon after, in 1243, by the Bavarians. The building had failed to fulfil Colonian hopes. It increased the power of the very neighbour it was meant to defy, and its value dwindled. Not even the energy of the new garrison helped much. By force of arms they did compel Adolf von Nassau to pay a toll on the way to his coronation in 1292, but by 1319, the castle was reduced to a widow's residence. It was never reinforced to withstand gunpowder and cannon, and only offered protection against the defenceless. In the Thirty Years' War, this was a base for marauding Spaniards, then for Swedes. In 1689, the French blew up all of it except for the tower. In 1993 Gernot Stelter acquired the castle ruin and began with its restoration. It can be viewed upon request.

Fürstenberg Ruin above Rheindiebach

## Stahleck Castle

Documentary evidence of the castle at Bacharach goes back to 1095. In 1142, it was the residence of the Counts Palatine of the Rhine, who were among the seven Electors of German Kings. And kings and emperors were guests at Stahleck. In 1194, it was scene of a peace-sealing marriage between the hostile Hohenstaufen and Guelphs. In 1214, both the office of Count Palatine and the castle passed to the Wittelsbachs. Their new residence had been the most important Rhine castle in the 12th century already. Even Charles IV did reverence to its beauty: that splendour-loving monarch, who made a "Golden City" of Prague, married at Stahleck in 1349. This is indicative of the unprecedented magnificence of the structure. In 1386, the Counts Palatine moved their centre of operations to Heidelberg, but the fortifications at Stahleck were kept up-to-date. When the French destroyed the Rhine castles in 1689, there was a huge stock of gunpowder in its casemates, enough to blast all castle and palace wings. Of this most valuable castle structure on the Rhine not even a ruin remained. In 1925/27, a youth hostel was erected on the foundations of Stahleck, and the remarkable townscape of Bacharach could only benefit from its lively silhouette.

Stahleck Castle (1095) above Bacharach

# Bacharach

It takes many ingredients to make an enchanting spot like Bacharach. Here, we could start with the location, for the little town snuggles up before the entrance to the wine-grown Steeger Valley, extending far into the wide Rhine Valley. And then, Bacharach can tap its historical past. The town was the medieval residence of one of the seven Electors, and of the most representative, in fact: the Count Palatine of the Rhine who, in the periods between the death of one German King and the coronation of the next, acted as "Imperial Vicar", steward of royal power. Thirdly, the town has many fine structures in close proximity. Here, in a nutshell, is a millennium of German cultural history. Fourthly, Bacharach has been blessed by nature with a good climate and with hill slopes that have produced a highly commended wine since time immemorial. It is a hospitable town, and beautiful, too. When Stahleck Castle was still there and the Werner Chapel was still intact, when all the handsome half-timber houses of yesteryear that went up in flames in the 1872 conflagration were still unscathed, Bacharach must indeed have been as captivating as an age-old fairy tale. What has largely survived is the **town wall** of 1344. With its towers and wall passages, it encompassed Stahleck Castle, too. From the outside, **St. Peter's** Evangelical parish church looks smaller than it is. Only the prominent tower

Bacharach, the "Old House" (1368)

Bacharach, Werner Chapel and St. Peter's parish church

contradicts this impression. The interior is a surprise. The Romanesque basilica with its three naves, galleries and enlarged Late Gothic windows has preserved its old colour. Dominating element is a huge 14th-century Christopher. The Catholic parish church of **St. Nicholas**, 1700, stands on the old toll bastion. The town still has splendid buildings aplenty. The Alte Post, Alte Münze, the Palatine cellarage, now the Town Hall, testify to this. The true marvel at Bacharach, however, is the **Werner Chapel**, set in the vineyard slopes. Started in 1290, this is one of the chief specimens of Rhenish Gothic. Damaged when Stahleck was blown up and shaken by a landslide, the chapel has been a ruin without vaulting or roof since 1787. Its filigree network of gleaming red sandstone is an unforgettable vision of loveliness.

Bacharach, Stahleck Castle and view of the town

## Gutenfels Castle

This name was only given to the castle above Kaub in 1504. That was when Landgrave William of Hesse was forced to break off his 45-day long siege of castle and town, during which he had bombarded them with over 1,200 stone and iron cannonballs. Legend attributes their deliverance to a brave burgher's daughter, Else Welzer, whose good deed is commemorated every year in a costume piece, "Elslein von Kaub". The castle, formerly called plain "Cube", meaning Kaub, was renamed "Gutenfels" by its grateful lord. It had been a Falkenstein property around 1200, but was sold along with the town to the Counts Palatine in 1277. The latter were after a source of ready cash as lucrative as the Rhine tolls at Bacharach. Following the construction of the toll-collecting fort on the island in the Rhine, Kaub Castle became a bone of contention, but remained the property of the Counts. After the Hessians had their work cut out with it, it was fought over by Swedes and Spaniards in the Thirty Years' War. That meant damage. Once patched together, it served as a home for disabled veterans until 1803. Napoleon gave orders for it to be sold for scrap, but again a deliverer was at hand. The present owner tends this well-preserved building from the days of the Hohenstaufen, now a castle hotel, for the benefit of posterity.

Gutenfels Castle above Kaub

# Kaub and the Pfalz in the Rhine

In the course of the construction of Gutenfels Castle, Kaub treated itself to a town wall in 1200, the object being to protect both its own and others' property. In those days, valuable cargoes were transferred to drays above the Binger Loch and conveyed by horse and cart from Rüdesheim to Kaub. This earned both towns a lot of money over the centuries. Kaub added the rich slate quarries in 1355. This early prosperity is still visible today, above all in the town's stately houses. One of them, with a Romanesque gable, is 650 years old. The cellars of old houses are often above the ground on account of the annual high water

The Pfalz in the Rhine near Kaub

levels, so that the ground floors are reached by stairs. Kaub's richest and biggest half-timber building is certainly the **"Goldener Hirsch"**, 1575. Also important is the former inn, **"Stadt Mannheim"**, 1780, with genuine old fabric wall coverings. **Blücher** slept here – after pursuing Napoleon as far as the Rhine. It was on New Year's Eve, 1813/14, that he ventured the memorable Rhine crossing with 100,000 Prussian soldiers over a bridge of barges. Blücher's quarters in Kaub are now a museum with many mementoes of his times. Near the memorial to "Marshall Forward" is the **Kauber Pegel**, the most important water gauge for Rhine shipping between Mainz and Cologne. The town's

**Parish Church** has gone through every architectural style since Romanesque, rising like a bulwark from the town wall and divided to serve both main denominations. The island in the Rhine before Kaub has narrowed the river to a bowshot. The Counts Palatine, good businessmen as they were, saw their chance and started charging a toll. First, they built a tower on the island, like the Mäuseturm before the Binger Loch. In 1338, they converted the building to make a complete toll castle, Pfalzgrafenstein, known today as the "Pfalz". It resembles a ship of stone with a sharp stem, parting ice floes and high water. Location and design of the Pfalz betray the perspicacity of a genius. In the 650 years of its history, it never fell to an enemy. Nor was it every necessary

Kaub, Gutenfels Castle and the Pfalz in the Rhine

to alter it. Only the outer walls were strengthened, most recently just before 1750. That was when the roofs and tower hood were given their delightful present-day form. The interior is open to the public. The living space available to the inmates of old is less than we find in modern submarines. Yet, for all the confined space, the Pfalz has a narrow, winding inner court adorned in summer by modest plant life.

# Oberwesel

"Town of Wine and Towers" is how Oberwesel sees itself. In vino veritas. And with 18 surviving towers of its original 21, Oberwesel is certainly unsurpassed on the Middle Rhine. The ringwall erected in 1216 was what once ensured the freedom of this town that can proudly boast of having been a **free imperial city**, as from 1257, just like Cologne, Frankfurt and Nuremberg. But not for long. In 1390/91, it took up arms to defend that freedom. In vain. And the "Wesel War" is only worthy of note because this was the first time cannon was used on the Rhine. Besides its **town wall**, Oberwesel has two very famous churches. The red Church of Our Lady (**Liebfrauenkirche**), 1308/51, contains one of

Oberwesel, view on the town

the oldest and finest altar shrines in all Germany, 1331, and outstanding choir stalls carved by the same hand. Of an equally high standard is the Late Gothic rood screen. The white **St. Martin's** Church was built, just after Our Lady, at the town's highest point. The huge west tower, 1435, served as corner bastion in the town wall. This church, too, is richly endowed with art treasures. In spite of heavy losses in the Thirty Years' War, at the hands of the French in 1689, and from conflagrations, Oberwesel is still one of Germany's compactest and most beautiful historical towns.

## Schönburg Castle

This castle on the steep cone at Oberwesel was bestowed in 1116 by Barbarossa on one of his henchmen who took his name from it. It became the seat of a large family, with each branch building its own residential quarters and keep. Which is how Schönburg Castle came to have 6 towers. The Rhine tolls made them rich, but it was the Oberwesel churches that were dear to their hearts. They were protected by the

Schönburg Castle near Oberwesel

strongest curtain-wall on the Rhine. One of them, Frederick by name, saw the world: he was brother-in-arms to a member of the House of Orange, Marshal of France, War Minister in Berlin, commander of the British army in Ireland. Made "Marshal of Schomburg", he fell in battle at the age of 73. That was in 1689, when the French burnt down his ancestral castle on the Rhine. 30 years later, the family was extinct. The castle has been restored, but without all those towers, and now houses a delightful hotel.

# Loreley

The Middle Rhine Valley narrows to the eye of a needle at the Loreley rock, a lump of slate all of 130 metres high and virtually perpendicular, obstructing the current and squeezing the river to a quarter of its natural girth. The Rhine becomes a torrent, being hindered as well by the rocks in the river bed. Full daylight penetrates this gorge for a few hours only. Thunder generates booming echoes, producing an

Loreley, slate rock (more than 130 metres high)

unforgettable spectacle of Nature Unbound, a prospect that horrified and terrified the bargees of old who had to propel their boats and barges without mechanical power. Now, the perfidies of Nature have ever tended to take on human guise in legend and folk tale. Here, too, we are told that a blonde nymph used to sit atop the rock and allure passing sailors with her feminine charms and siren-song. The men gazed up at the Loreley instead of heeding the perilous waters and duly came to grief on the rocks. The story was retold by poet Heinrich

Heine and put to music by Friedrich Silcher, making it the world's first rock song. What escaped the poet's notice is that the southern slope is a vineyard. Visitors to the summit will find both the remnants of a Celtic rampart and an open-air theatre. Blondes can still be found there in summer, but of a more wholesome kind.

Loreley, the legendary slate rock

## Katz Castle

The quiet village bearing the fairy-tale name of Katzenelnbogen is located in the Taunus Hills, but the family of counts that erected an ancestral castle here in 1095 was in no mood for fairy-tales but for power and wealth. The lords of the castle with the odd name lost no time in finding a source of same. The Rhine was the road to riches in those days, and the family set about finding a lucrative perch on the river. After a ninety-year wait, fortune smiled, and the Counts of Katzenelnbogen reached the Rhine in 1185. A no longer surviving valley fort came into their possession in St. Goar. For a toll station the location was right, but not the size and strength of the building. The construction of Rheinfels Castle high above St. Goar solved the problem for the time being. But the Rhine is rather wide at this point and cannot be fully controlled from the left bank alone. A base on the right bank, too, was imperative, if all passing ships were to be stopped to pay toll. Count William II found a suitable site up the hill over St. Goarshausen and started erecting a new fortified toll station there in 1360. This paid off so well that its builder had the name of the ancestral castle transferred to it. He called it affectionately Neukatzenelnbogen, which was just too long for popular usage, and Cat Castle (Burg Katz) went

St. Goarshausen and Katz Castle

down much better. With their toll barrier between St. Goarshausen and St. Goar, the Counts of Katzenelnbogen managed to fall in line between the Counts Palatine and the Archbishops of Trier to join the chief beneficiaries of Rhine trade. Thanks to their castles of Rheinfels and Katz they could no longer be eliminated from the toll business. This success whetted their appetite for further income of the same sort, and we will meet them again as temporary owners of Marksburg Castle, which they acquired by purchase. When the Counts of Katzenelnbogen died out, the Katz fell to their heirs, the Landgraves of Hesse. By 1700, the castle had fallen into decay, not without the help of zealous French castle smashers. And in 1806, the Katz was reduced to a tower stump. Its reconstruction, 1896/98, was only made possible by the precise survey carried out in 1608 by the Hessian master builder Dilich. Only the tower was not given is original height, and remained a ruin. Katz Castle has been privately owned since 1989 and cannot be viewed

▽ Katz Castle above St. Goarshausen    In the Valley of the Loreley and Katz Castle ▷

## St. Goarshausen

Below the Loreley Rock, the Rhine settles down. While it was still agitated, it was alive with salmon. As late as 1900, the pink meat of the Rhine salmon was a must on the menus of the big passenger steamers. One millennium previously, St. Goarshausen had been a fishing village. At this point, before the Loreley rapids, the salmon assembled on their way up the Rhine to their spawning grounds. The place was acquired by the Counts of Katzenelnbogen in 1284. It became a town in 1324 and was given a town wall, as is right and proper. Following the construction of Katz Castle, the wall was extended up that far, and even enclosed the vineyards. These latter are of vital importance to the hospitable town, which has lost its fishing. The town's main street has always run parallel to the river bank, so it used to get along with only two gates, each guarded by a strong tower. The towers have survived, but gates and walls largely vanished. Neat half-timber houses on the main street and in the Burggasse are a vivid reminder of a medieval town. Its culture is reflected in the big Trinity painted by Lucas Cranach in the Catholic parish church. Recent extensions to the town make use of narrow valleys, made by rivulets descending from the Taunus Hills to the Rhine, to link up with the plateau, which is the only place where the town can grow. The Old Town is the gateway to the Loreley-Burgen-Strasse which escorts the Rhine along the brink from Lorch to Kamp-Bornhofen and opens up regularly to provide exciting glimpses of faraway places and the course of the Rhine Valley.

St. Goarshausen, Rhine Promenade and Katz Castle

St. Goarshausen, Rhine Panorama

St, Goarshausen, the „Rhein in Flammen" (firework display)

## St. Goar

Goar's name betrays its Celtic origin. Some time around 550 A. D., that pious man came to Germany from the south of France to convert the local heathen, and why he opted for this point along the Rhine Valley is not hard to guess. This was where the mariners surviving the Loreley rapids used to make their offerings to their gods. And the amounts they pledged might just as well go to Christian patron saints. The Celt became Saint Goar, and his tomb was a place of pilgrimage by 650. A monastery looked after the pilgrims. In 1185, the Counts of Katzenelnbogen assumed the stewardship over the monastery, pocketing the little valley fort of St. Goar at the same time, first of all as head office. This gave them a toehold on the banks of the Rhine. The construction of the town wall before 1219 included a site for the Rheinfels castle to be built later on the hill. Sheltered by the castle, the town flourished. The collegiate church of St. Goar rose over the splendid 11th-century crypt. Fine Late Gothic net vaulting was added when the building was enlarged to make a hall-shaped residence church just before the counts' family died out in 1479. It was richly decorated. The building is now Evangelical Parish Church. The town's houses, too, improved in quality, and a good number of the historic burghers' houses have survived. When Rheinfels Castle was embel-lished to become a residence around 1580, handicrafts enjoyed a heyday. Repeated sieges of town and castle

Katz Castle above St. Goarshausen, vis-a-vis St. Goar and Rheinfels Castle

St. Goar, Rhine Panorama and ferryboat

St. Goar and Rheinfels Castle

in 1255/56 and 1322 did cause some damage, and the Thirty Years' War left its mark as well. Yet, even the tough siege by the French in 1692 failed to destroy the town. Indeed, it was a citizen by the name of Kretsch who caused the French to withdraw. This member of the rifle guild took aim at the French general, Tallard, from the tower of the church, and hit him. Taking its seriously wounded chief, the whole army, 28,000 strong, took to its heels. In addition to the grave slab of St. Goar, a masterpiece of the period around 1330, the Neogothic Catholic Parish Church houses one of the country's finest altar paintings of the outgoing Middle Ages. The hospitable town is linked to a **network of hiking trails**, and its good inns and a lot of houses offering accommodation make it a centre of tourism on the Middle Rhine. On the third Saturday in September, the castles for miles around are illuminated, and the great firework display, "Rhein in Flammen", offers visitors to the river an impressive spectacle.

Rheinfels Castle (1245) above St. Goar ▷

## Rheinfels Castle

In 1245, Count Dieter V of Katzenelnbogen started building Rheinfels Castle above St. Goar. The Taunus lord did not have to skimp. The old valley castle below the new site had been charging tolls for 60 years, but its walls no longer offered the necessary security. The counts, however, since the construction of their Hohenstein Castle in the Taunus Hills, 1190, were now castle experts and well on the way to becoming masters of their craft and second to none. The plans on display in the castle museum show how the builders made full use of the spur of rock bearing the new castle and what alterations they made to render it impregnable. It was not long before the building had to prove its worth. Once completed, the lords of the castle drastically increased the toll rates, and that brought the League of Rhine Cities on the scene. The populace was mobilized and the castle besieged for one year, 1255/56. But they did not capture the castle, and there was no more talk of cutting the tolls. The proceeds financed generous residential reconstruction and, after 1332, the keep was heightened and given the churn shape that Marksburg Castle over Braubach still has. This was typical

of the buildings of the Counts of Katzenelnbogen. The tower of Katz Castle, too, used to look that way. A new hall brought more comfort. Women's apartments were added. Any other ambitious plans of the Counts stopped there, for the family died out in 1479. Heirs were the Landgraves of Hesse who started, in 1480/1527, by making a fortress of the castle. Outworks in front of the castle walls and casemates on the inside made the whole into what was then a modern fortified structure.

Further conversions in 1570/80 produced a princely residence with magnificent interiors and gables with rich Renaissance half-timbering. The women's apartments of the Counts of Katzenelnbogen became a vaulted chapel. By 1667, the fortifications had again been strengthened. Its redoubts, forts and ravelins in Baroque fortification style made Rheinfels into one of Germany's strongest fortresses. In 1692, 4,000 defenders defied a French army of 28,000. Its end came in 1792,

Rheinfels Castle above St. Goar

when its commander handed it over to the French without a struggle. And they blew up all they could: keep, hall, outworks. The ruin became a quarry. In 1843, it was acquired by the later Emperor William I. Restoration started in 1925, but some idea of the size and beauty of Rheinfels may be had from the model of the fortress and pictures by the architect, Dilich, 1607/08, both on show in the castle museum. A tour of the huge castle will reveal its dimensions, and a visit to the museum round off the picture. No other castle on the Rhine discloses so much of its structure and workings, quite apart from its history. The conducted tour lasts one and a half hours.

Rheinfels Castle above St. Goar

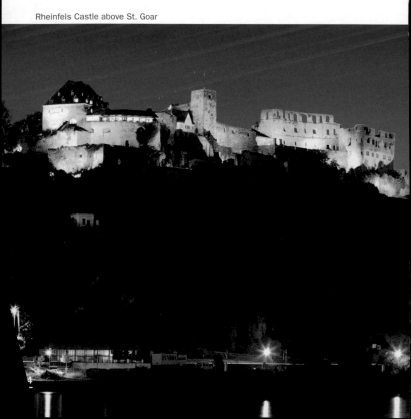

## Maus Castle

In 1255, the rhine cities took a stand against the counts from the Taunus because they were the privilege of the Electors. The latter feared for their vested interests. Directly affected were the Electors of Trier, and so, scarcely ten years after Rheinfels Castle was completed, the Archbishop of Trier was building a new castle of his own over the little town of Wellmich on the right bank. Small but insidious, it faced the lords of St. Goar. "Peterseck" it was called then "Deuernburg". Trier's archbishops, Kuno of Falkenstein and Werner of Königstein, uncle and nephew, liked living here, and this was where they died, in 1388 and 1418. The Katzenelnbogeners had responded at once with a much bigger castle, "the Cat" (die Katz), started 1371. This highlighted the imbalance of power, and the bishops' castle was ridiculed as "Mouse Castle" (Burg Maus). The name caught the popular fancy and has stuck. It was auctioned for quarrying in 1806, but later restored by private interests and houses a marvelous eagle and falcon farm with free-flight bird shows and lectures.

Maus Castle above Wellmich

## Kamp-Bornhofen

**Kamp** is the older section of this double municipality. Mentioned in documents prior to 950, it was part of the "Boppard Empire", the biggest coherent Imperial estate on the Middle Rhine, which the quarrelsome Archbishop Balduin, brother of Emperor Henry VII of the House of Luxemburg, brought under Trier's control after 1300. This state of affairs continued till 1802. In its Neo-Romanesque parish church, Kamp still has the tombs and altar table of the former Early Gothic church. It, too, was consecrated to the patron saint of mariners, St. Nicholas. The younger district, **Bornhofen**, gained ascendancy as a place of pilgrimage, even before 1289. For 700 years now, pilgrims have been doing reverence to the miraculous image, the still highly revered Pietà. It was to serve it and to look after pilgrims that the **Monastery of Bornhofen** was founded in 1679. The pilgrimage chapel (**Gnadenkapelle**), 1691, was added to the church, which had been consecrated in 1435. This gives a delightfully winding layout to the double-nave hall building. Kamp-Bornhofen is the starting-point of the Loreley-Burgen-Strasse over the peripheral hills of the Taunus. It links a number of particularly interesting castles and fine vantage-points. For the rest, Kamp-Bornhofen is well equipped to accommodate and provide for the physical well-being of close on thousands of guests. The town is easy to reach by the B 42, the road along the right bank of the Rhine. In summer, there are good boat connections to other points on the river. A car ferry links Boppard with this double town below its two famous castles (the "Hostile Brothers", Sterrenberg and Liebenstein).

Kamp-Bornhofen

## The Hostile Brothers

The rocky ridge at the back of Bornhofen bears the ruins of two castles. These are separated by a high wall known locally as the **Fighting Wall**. And thereby hangs a tale. At Sterrenberg Castle, we are told, there once lived a knight, whose consort died young. After that, a young damsel kept the house for him and his two growing sons. The latter lost their hearts to the girl, and the younger of the two found favour

with her. One day, recruiting started for a crusade, and the lucky lad was off to the Holy Land, the damsel having pledged her troth. On his return after many years, however, the lad brought a Greek wife with him. Sterrenberg Senior built a new home for the couple and called it Liebenstein Castle. The elder brother was dismayed at the younger's faithlessness, and soon a high wall separated the two premises. Yet, the brothers met in church, and swords were drawn. In a vain attempt to separate them, the damsel was stabbed and died. The two brothers fell in a duel, and all of this broke the father's heart. So much for legend. History tells a different tale. **Sterrenberg** was an imperial castle even before 1100 and was a fief of the lords of Bolanden in 1195. They

The Hostile Brothers above Kamp-Bornhofen

added a gatehouse, and the result was **Liebenstein Castle**, around 1200. Over one hundred years later, Bornhofen passed to the Electors of Trier along with Sterrenberg Castle. But not so Liebenstein Castle, and the Fighting Wall was built as an extra shield. After 1550, Trier let Sterrenberg Castle fall into decay, and Liebenstein Castle was given up in 1600. Sections of the two ruins are now roofed over again, and there are hostelries inviting visitors to sit back and enjoy the view.

# Boppard

About 50 A. D., the Romans built a castrum upstream from the biggest loop made by the Rhine. Its name, Bodobrica, was borrowed from an older Celtic settlement on the same site. Following the incursions of the Alemannians in 350, a three-metre thick town wall was erected in the typical Roman rubblework fashion. The wall had 28 round towers, and the eleven still surviving are 10 m high. So, Boppard has the best preserved Roman town wall in Germany. Further out, there is a 12th-century town wall as well, which was fortified and extended by castle

Boppard

and tollhouse after the Imperial town of Boppard was annexed by Archbishop Balduin of Trier in 1327. The present-day townscape is quite steeped in history. The narrow streets of the Old Town are crowded with churches, monasteries, noble houses and burghers' homes. The castle, itself town history, houses the Civic Museum. The proud church of **St. Severus** with its twin towers dominating the town dates back to an early Christian structure that had risen from the ruins of the Baths of the withdrawing Romans. The present building, 1200, is the fourth church to be erected on this site. Of its predecessor only the mighty towers have survived. The church is a three-nave vaulted basilica with galleries. Space before the choir is confined. This is where the two towers project into the church, which then widens again toward the choir, so that the whole is longer in perspective than it really is. The medieval colour scheme of the beautiful interior has been preserved or renewed. The Late Romanesque crucifix over the High Altar is its most valuable artistic treasure. Worth visiting, too, is the **Carmelite Church**, started soon after 1300, spireless, vaulted in after 1440. It boasts fine murals dated 1407, and is rich in sculpture of a high standard. From its earliest days dates the **"Traubenmadonna"**, which winegrowers every year present with grapes (Trauben) that are left to dry up at her feet. Also of interest are the tomb figures from Dürer's time, true masterpieces of portrait sculpture. In addition to its old architecture and sculpture, Boppard is blessed with a fine location in the landscape. Downstream, the left bank produces the most top wine on the Middle Rhine, the vineyards extending for kilometres in the intense southern sun. Upstream, half way up the slope, you can walk along the primeval riverbed as far as Bad Salzig. It was as much as 100 metres higher than the present bed. Up here is where Engelbert Humperdinck lived: friend of Wagner and late Romantic composer of "Hänsel and Gretel". The slope is a real feast for the eyes in cherry blossom time and a delight for the palate at harvest time. From Boppard station, the Hunsrückbahn lifts passengers to the Hunsrück Hills, 400 metres higher up. And there's a chair lift to take them in a few minutes to the Four Lake Vista **(Vierseenblick)**. From this magnificent vantage-point, the winding course of the Rhine, intersected by lines of hills, looks like a chain of lakes. The great loop made by the river, the "Bopparder Hamm", appears to enclose the

Boppard, Rhine Panorama

Four Lake Vista above Boppard

roundish hills on the right bank and make an island of them. An expansive landscape, indeed, and doubly astonishing to anyone who has just emerged from the narrow confines of the Rhine Valley.

Boppard, view of the town

# Braubach

King Rudolph of Habsburg granted the town its charter in 1276. A town wall was then built, and extended to join the one hundred year old castle. The settlement itself is much older, however, being mentioned in 691. **St. Martin's** church at the cemetery is ancient. Seven years after receiving its charter, both Braubach and **Marksburg Castle** passed to the Counts of Katzenelnbogen. The toll rights caught their fancy, and so they extended the citadel over the town to include a toll station within reach of the river. This old valley castle was replaced in 1568 by the new Philippsburg. Among the decorative remains are the half-timber gables. Medieval town fortifications include the striking tower of the **Barbarakirche** (church), the **Pankgrafenturm** (tower) and the **Obertor** (gate). Ruins of fortified towers and town wall, too, have survived, as have half-timber houses giving living testimony of former life styles. The former Barbarakirche, now Evangelical community centre, was consecrated to the patron saint of miners, a fact that is due to the local silver mines, first mentioned in 1301. The church has Gothic wall paintings. The three-sided gallery with its splendid carved parapet was a present of the Reformation, 1580. For the tourist, present-day Boppard is a town of wine and roses. 150 metres above Braubach is Marksburg Castle. Half way up the hill is the Martinskapelle with a fine view of castle and river.

Braubach, Old Town Gate

# Marksburg Castle

The castle owes its name to its patron saint, St. Mark, and the chapel in the oldest tower is consecrated to him. For over 800 years, he has warded off the fate that befell all other high castles on the Rhine: conquest and destruction. The castle is not a homogeneous structure, and many expert hands have worked on it. The founder, one of the nobles of Braubach, had an eye for the strategic position of the perch he settled on in 1150. The point can be attacked neither from the Rhine side nor from the back. After 1200, the castle was occupied by vassals of the Counts Palatine. Eberhard of Eppstein had extended and fortified it by 1219. In the middle of the triangular castle yard he erected a square keep, the entrance accessible by an eight-metre long ladder. The castle chapel was housed in a tower of its own. A Romanesque hall was built on the north side of the castle, which now gained in space, luxury and strength. In 1283, Marksburg Castle was acquired by the Counts of Katzenelnbogen, who impeded access to the castle yard by building a gatehouse and further gates on the twisting road up to the main building. A wolf-trap was installed before one of the gates. Once the bridge over it was raised, any attackers fell in and were impaled. All the castle buildings were surrounded by a fortified enclosing wall with the outer bailey behind. The square keep was heightened by the new owners with the addition of a round slender element to produce the churn shape characteristic of all Katzenelnbogen castles. And they joined a second hall building in Gothic style

Marksburg Castle above Braubach

on to the chapel tower, with a three-metre thick outer wall letting the light in as through shafts, for this is the side of the castle open to attack. The building is a double-storey structure with a 6 x 24 metres room on each floor serving as banqueting halls. The counts resided in the castle for a time, and for this purpose it was fortified again about 1400. The chapel tower was heightened. A second, outer wall much further out now enclosed the gatehouse and the gradually sloping outlying land at the back. The last Count of Katzenelnbogen died in 1479. His heirs, the Landgraves of Hesse, still did not feel quite safe enough in Marksburg Castle. The fine location did protect its walls from direct bombardment, but approaching infantry ought to be repelled with cannon. After 1500, therefore, the Hessians set up the Gun House, the forward salient of the "Sharp Corner" and the mighty "Powder Corner" to deal with attackers from the Dachsenhausen valley at the back. A major and a minor battery were installed, and the whole investment paid off. In 1689/92, when the French went round burning down Rhine castles, Marksburg Castle remained intact, and that was the way the Prussians took it over in 1866. In 1899, it passed to the German Castles Association, which has its headquarters here. A tour of the castle covers not only the citadel, but includes the impressive castle kitchen in the Gothic hall building. And anyone interested in medieval justice should not miss the torture chamber in the cellar of the older hall building, where he will find a whole arsenal of instruments of torture and chastisement. The next stop should be the castle inn, housed in a building especially designed in period style. It is situ-

Battery Courtyard

ated just behind the drawbridge gate and is roomy enough to cope with the busiest of days.

Marksburg Castle above Braubach „Rhein in Flammen"

## Lahnstein

This town is a recent product obtained by combining two older towns with quite different pasts. Even before the year 1000, **Oberlahnstein** was the northernmost base of the Electoral Archbishops of Mainz. **Niederlahnstein**, on the other hand, had grown out of a Roman castrum at the mouth of the Lahn. Originally an Imperial possession, it passed to the Electorate of Trier in 1016, and was given an important **John the Baptist church**. Its high tower dominated the Rhine bank below the mouth of the Lahn. With a citadel, the Lahneck, with Martinsburg

Oberlahnstein, Martinsburg Palace (around 1300)

Castle on the Rhine and its strong town wall, Oberlahnstein became the stronghold of the area. **Lahneck Castle**, picturesquely perched on a ridge, was built by the princes of Mainz in 1240/45 to protect a silver mine. Burned down by the French in 1688, it was rebuilt in Neogothic style, starting in 1854, and refurnished true to period. **Martinsburg Castle** was the cornerstone of the town wall and guarantor of Mainz's dominion. Around 1300, it became toll station to replace rebellious Boppard and was a rich source of revenue for Mainz. Worth visiting in this part of town are the considerable remains of the **old town wall**, the hall and court of the Archbishopric of Mainz, about 1160, and the delightful Town Hall, a Late Gothic half-timbered building. The young

Oberlahnstein, Lahneck Castle (1240)

twin town of Lahnstein has a new hot spring together with a Kurhaus on the hill. Before the "Wirtshaus an der Lahn" is a pavilion from Baroque times on the stone blocks of a medieval ice-breaker. Lahnstein's location at the point of intersection of four regions of wooded hills, viz. the Eifel, Hunsrück, Taunus and Westerwald, makes the town an ideal starting and finishing point for walking and motoring tours, with ample facilities for fortifying oneself before and after.

Niederlahnstein, Wirtshaus an der Lahn (1697)

## Stolzenfels Palace

The much celebrated castle opposite the mouth of the Lahn was built
by Trier. No sooner had the Electorate of Mainz barricaded the mouth
of the Lahn valley with Lahneck Castle, than the Electorate of Trier ap-
peared with a "castle" of its own on the chessboard of power. Only ten
years after Mainz's Lahneck Castle, Trier's Stolzenfels Castle too was
completed. And as soon as Mainz started charging tolls at Lahnstein in
1300, Trier followed suit with the toll station at the foot of Stolzenfels
Castle. The toll tower built for this purpose on the river bank fell victim
to railway construction 130 years ago. In 1688/89, the French burned
the castle down in the course of their siege of Koblenz. The ruin was
gifted in 1823 by Koblenz to the Prussian Crown Prince, later King
Frederick William IV. The latter commissioned the Prussian senior di-
rector of public works, Karl Friedrich Schinkel, to restore the castle.
The order ran: conservation. As far as the Rhine side is concerned,
Schinkel obeyed: keep, square fortress-house tower and twin-aisle hall
building were preserved in their masonry. The hill side was redesigned,
and chapel and gateway are from Schinkel's time. But the hand of an
architect of European stature made of Stolzenfels Palace a masterpiece
of Romantic building art on German soil. The quality of the buildings
is reflected in the interior. The painting of many rooms, excellent furniture and art collections often moved the royal builder to reside with his
consort in this magnificently situated castle. Present-day visitors, too,
will enjoy traversing its banqueting halls.

Stolzenfels Palace, vis-a-vis the Mouth of the Lahn

## Koblenz

The town's name is of Roman origin. Augustus' rampart fort was destroyed in 70 A. D. A town wall from the end of the 3rd century is still visible in parts, but it was no match for the onset of the Germanic tribes. After 400, the Franks set up a royal court in the Roman ruins. In 842 and 860, Charlemagne's heirs conferred in the church of **St. Kastor**, consecrated 830. The town was gifted to the Archbisho-

Koblenz, Deutsches Eck with Mouth of the Moselle

Koblenz, Deutsches Eck / Cavalier Monument Emperor Wilhelms I

pric of Trier in 1018. Business boomed, and a new courthouse was needed, along with further churches: **Liebfrauen** and **St. Florin**. Koblenz minted ducats. The wine trade flourished, and transport routes to the Rhine were necessary. In 1343, Elector Balduin's Moselle bridge of stone provided access by land for heavy casks. In 1430, the staple-house (**Kaufhaus**) was erected. Religious orders built schools and churches. Salients were protecting the town around 1600. Still, the Thirty Years' War cost it half its buildings. In 1688, the French bombarded it for weeks, but in vain, although serious damage was caused. In 1777, the last lord spiritual started building a castle on the bank of the Rhine, but it was never completed. In 1794, the builder fled before

Koblenz, Am Plan and the Church of Liebfrauen (12th century)

the advancing French, who annexed the town. In 1815, it passed to the Prussians and was developed into the strongest Rhine fortress, a role it lost in 1920. After losing 81 % of its buildings in World War II, Koblenz was capital of the State of Rhineland Palatinate till 1950. Since then, it has been a city. Canalization of the Moselle provided additional impetus. The town's road network is linked to three autobahns, viz. on either side of the Rhine for points south, and via Trier for foreign parts. War damage has been repaired wherever possible or given way to new buildings. Koblenz is again a town for strolling in. The Old Town has captivating streetscapes and squares: at the **"Am Plan"** with the view of the outlandish hoods of Liebfrauen, in the Löhrstraße and in front of the old staple-house. In the inner court of the former Jesuit college, now City Hall, there's a splashing fountain, the **Schängel-Brunnen**, commemorating a town scamp. In the wine village on the south side, Moselle and Rhine compete for the attention of the connoisseur. Wine, after all, has ever been the elixir of life in this town at "Deutsches Eck", the confluence of Rhine and Moselle, exhilerating both as wines and as rivers.

Koblenz, Schängel-Brunnon

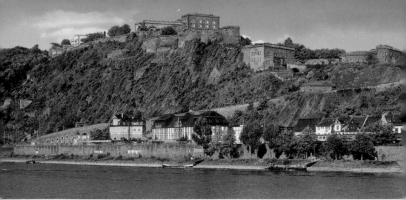

Koblenz, Ehrenbreitstein Fortress (around 1100)

## Der Ehrenbreitstein

Even before 1100, a noble builder by the name of Ehrenbert had built
a fort atop a cliff opposite the mouth of the Moselle. It was acquired in
1152 by the Electorate of Trier and expanded. Around 1500, the castle
became a fortress. Cologne folk hero and Imperial general Jan von
Werth had to win it back in 1636 from the French, who had been let
in by a treacherous Elector in 1631. In 1688, the French again desired
admittance, this time in vain. By 1750, the brilliant Balthasar Neumann
had made the fortress impregnable. Four French attacks were repelled,
1794/99. It was hunger that finally reduced it to submission. Immense
quantities of gunpowder were used to blow it up in 1801. In 1816/32,
Prussia did for Ehrenbreitstein all that military architecture of the day
could. The Treaty of Versailles brought demilitarization.

Koblenz, Ehrenbreitstein Fortress (around 1100) „Rhein in Flammen"

## Bendorf und Sayn Palace

The Middle Ages and modernity go hand in hand in Bendorf: the part of the town called Sayn and its castle transport the visitor back into the history of the County of Sayn. In the 13th century, Premonstratensian monks founded an **abbey** here. Even today, one can find traces of the past. The castle precincts contain an exhibition of tower clocks crafted by famous master builders. If you are looking for a cosy place to stop and rest awhile, then the castle tavern is just right. In 1848, the Neogothic **Palace of the Counts of Sayn-Wittgenstein** was constructed below the castle. Today one can see the restored Sayn Palace and the palace tower. The garden belonging to the castle is magnificent: colorful butterflies flutter amidst an exotic, dreamy landscape, fascinating young and old alike. The unity of the church ceased to be an issue in Bendorf long ago: the **Catholic and Protestant parish churches** are inseparably bound to one another by the bell tower. Today the tower, which dates from the year 1204, is property of the city, which also maintains the carillon. The bells ring out over the square in front of the churches four times a day. For those who want to experience modern history, the 19th century **"Sayner Hut"** is just the thing. The three-naved cast iron building was constructed by the Prussians as a state iron foundry.

Bendorf, Sayn Palace

## Neuwied

The area which is now Neuwied was already inhabited by the ancient Romans, who established a fortified outpost here. But the city itself was first founded in 1653 by the Count of Wied to replace the town of Langendorf, which was destroyed in the Thirty Years' War. Neuwied is protected from floods by massive dikes and a water level tower. The main sightseeing attraction in the heart of the well-preserved city is the **Palace** (17th century), which is situated in the park and was based on the palace at Versailles. The past comes alive in the historic downtown area as well: the **Herrnhuter Fraternal Community** (1783 – 85), **Mennonite Church** (1768) and County Museum are reminders of turbulent times. Nature lovers will find what they are after at the **Neuwieder Zoo**. The familiar and exotic animals are very popular with the visitors.

Neuwied Palace

Medieval Rhine Gate

Round Tower

# Andernach

Andernach looks back upon a long history. Founded as a Roman military outpost named "Antunnacum" 2,000 years ago, the former free imperial city was often fought over. In the 6th century, the town was mentioned as being the seat of the Franconian royal court. There are still many well-preserved architectural monuments in the heart of the city. The gates and towers of the **city wall** constructed in the 14th and 15th centuries are visible to the visitor from quite a distance, including the 15th century "Round Tower" (56 meter [ca. 183 feet] high). The legendary **"Andernacher Baker Boys"** are immortalized as stone figures in the partly Romanesque, partly Gothic Rhine Gate. The four towers of the Catholic Church of **St. Mary** ("St Mary's Cathedral"), built in 1198, rise above the town at the market square. The **Protestant parish church** on the east side of the market square dates from the 14th and 15th centuries. One sign of the town's turbulent history is the ruin of a **palace** once belonging to the Electorate of Cologne, now surrounded by public gardens, which was destroyed in 1689. Even modern buildings are already antiquated: the **"Old Crane"** at the end of the riverfront was used to unload millstones until 1911.

Andernach Castle

Andernach, Rhine Panorama

## Bad Breisig

The spa of Bad Breisig is bubbling over with good health. Soothing baths, massages, relaxing quite and gentle invigoration of bodies stressed by the rigors of everyday life await the guest. Just the thing against rheumatism, heart and kidney diseases or metabolic disorders, which can be healed the natural way in Bad Breisig. Six hundred meters (ca. 2,000 feet) down in the volcanic rock of the Eifel mountain range are **four Medicinal springs** which feed several thermal baths as warm

Bad Breisig, Half-timbered houses

Bad Breisig, Rhine panorama

geysers. The **Ludgerussprudel** spring feeds the bath house, the indoor pool is feed by the **Geiersprudel spring**, and the **Mariensprudel spring** emerges underneath the outdoor pool. An additional outdoor pool draws its curative power from the **Gertrudis spring**. Visitors can also find relaxation outside the spa area – the old heart of the city with its dreamy nooks and corners is also steeped in tranquillity. A charmingly situated, picturesque backdrop of residences from the 17th and 18th centuries extends along the banks of the Rhine. It is possible to stroll for more than six kilometers (ca. 3 3/4 miles) along the river. The 13th century **Catholic parish church of St. Victor** in "Upper Breisig" (Oberbreisig) contains precious frescos; in "Lower Breisig" (Niederbreisig), the **Church of the Ascension of St. Mary** (18th century) and lovely 17th and 18th century residences are open to the public. There are also attractions for young visitors to Bad Breisig: the **Doll Museum** and the **Storybook Forest** are popular places for excursions. Visible from far away, the 12th century **Rheineck Castle** looms high above the city. There are also idyllic places here where one can go for a walk. Every July, Bad Breisig turns into a Mecca for gourmets: a "Knight of the Culinary Round-Table" is crowned as part of the **"Culinary Week"**; there is also a gourmet buffet featuring specialities from all over the world. There is even a festival dedicated to the thermal springs. Each year, an elected queen commemorates the healing, bubbling water.

# Rheineck Castle

Located high above Bad Breisig, Rheineck Castle offers a beautiful view of the Rhine valley. The mighty fortress was built by the Count Palatine in the twelfth century and was misused by greedy robber barons as a refuge just a few years later. In 1151, King Conrad III recaptured the castle and had it burnt to the ground. Barbarossa's Chancellor Rainald of Dassel was the first to reconstruct the fortress for Electoral Cologne. In 1282, the castle was destroyed once again by King Rudolph of Habsburg dynasty. Thereafter the government of Electoral Cologne housed honourable financial administrators in the residence on the Rhine. Only the 20 meter (ca. 65 1/2 feet) high, square watchtower and the ruins of the chapel survived the destruction of the castle by the French in 1689. Years later, in 1832, Professor Moritz of Bethmann-Hollweg, member of a family of Frankfurt bankers, commissioned the Late-Romantic architect Johann Claudius of Lassaulx from Coblence to artfully restore Rheineck Castle. Now it is privately owned and cannot be viewed.

Rheineck Castle

Bad Hönningen, health resort garden

## Bad Hönningen

Bad Hönningen is considered to be the **"Gateway to Rhine-Wester-wald Wildlife Park"**. Hikers can have an impressive experience of nature amongst the shady woods, sleepy valleys, babbling brooks or secluded ponds. Alongside relaxation in the great outdoors, the spa also offers expert treatment. In the **Thermal bath**, mineral-rich water helps provide relief for rheumatism, heart disease or circulatory disorders. One can go for a dip in both the indoor (31° C / 87.8° F) and outdoor (26° – 28° C [78.8° – 82.4° F]) pools. For a rest afterward, try the sunbathing lawn right next to the Rhine, the well-manicured spa park or the extensive Rhine promenades. Massages, physical therapy and medicinal baths round out the spa offerings in Bad Hönningen. The thermal springs not only have a healing function, but are also used to produce carbon dioxide. The pedestrian zone adds a modern touch to the partially historical heart of the city. Visitors can find the romance typical of the Rhine in the Ariendorf section of town with its chapel and the old half timbered buildings. In the vicinity, there are several **Cloister courtyards** dating from the 18th century.

Arenfels Palace

## Arenfels Palace near Bad Hönningen

The mighty fortress of Arenfels was built by one Lord of Isenburg around 1259. After the Arenfels branch of the builder's family died out in 1371, the castle changed hands repeatedly. With time, two round towers were erected next to the early Gothic castle precincts. The construction could no longer be used as a defensible castle, however, because the hill on which it was situated was too low. Thus the entire castle was rebuilt as a palace and fitted out with magnificent Renaissance and early Baroque pediments. Count of Westerholt Arenfels purchased the castle in 1824, but then allowed it to deteriorate under the direction of the Cologne Cathedral builder Zwirner. By 1951, the vast arsenal of weapons, the furniture and the precious library had all been auctioned off. Today the castle is privately owned and is dosed to the public with the exception of the castle restaurant. The castle is situated below the spa Bad Hönningen and can be conveniently reached via footpaths. Hiking trails all around Arenfels promise hours of relaxation.

# Linz

Linz was first mentioned in official documents in 874. Around 1320, Linz was granted the rights of a city; it belonged to the Electorate of Cologne until 1803. The partially preserved fortification walls and city gates were built using native basalt. Even today, Linz is one of the main transshipment centers for the basalt quarried in the vicinity. The city was besieged and occupied several times in its history. The market in the old city forms the focus of the picturesque town. Here one can see colorful half-timbered buildings, uncovered in the twenties, which span five centuries and have given the city the nickname **"Colorful City on the Rhine"**. In 1365, the Archbishop of Cologne built the **Citadel and toll castle "Feith"** in the lower part of the city. Until the beginning of 19th century, Linz was one of eleven tariff stations between Cologne and Mainz. In addition, the castle also served as the summer residence of the Archbishop of Cologne. Today the castle contains an exhibition of **automated mechanical musical instruments** from three centuries and, in the castle dungeon, medieval instruments of torture; there is a discotheque in the tower. The **oldest city hall in the State of Rhineland-Palatinate** dates from the year 1392. A carillon plays various melodies three times each day. Half-timbered buildings are still being built or lovingly restored in Linz. Bronze and stone figures commemorate old customs: the **"Klapperjunge"** in front of the New Gate, symbolic of an old Holy Saturday custom, the market woman

Linz, Castle Square

"Agnes" at the Butter Market or the **"Linzer Strünzer"** or "exaggerator", a pictorial symbol for the inhabitants of Linz, who are given to exaggeration. The valuable frescos in the late Romanesque **Church of St. Martin** (consecrated in 1214) are an unforgettable experience for any art lover. In the late 15th century, Tilmann Joel, chancellor and adviser to the electors and archbishops, sponsored construction of a Ratskapelle or "town chapel" with an altar of St. Mary for his hometown of Linz. Today, the famous altar triptych hangs in the new **Parish church of St. Mary**. Ockenfels Castle and Dattenberg Castle are situated high above the city. The home of the full-bodied red wines of Ahr lies directly opposite from Linz on the other side of the Rhine: this is where the Ahr River flows into the Rhine. But Linz is also considered to be a town with good wine – one of the largest and most popular wine festivals on the Rhine is held here every September. Linz also lives up to its reputation as a "colorful city" in social life. For a few days each year in early summer, the city becomes a meeting place for organ grinders from all over the world during the "Colorful Week". In May, the section of the Rhine between Linz and Bonn is transformed into a colorful sea of light with a huge fireworks display **("The Rhine in Flames")**.

Linz, Rhine Panorama

82

## Remagen

The Celts were the first people to settle in the vicinity of the modern city of Remagen, but the Romans were the first to set up a military outpost here ("Rigomagus"). The naive of the old 11th century Romanesque church now forms the basis for the vestibule of the Neo-Romanesque **Catholic parish church of Sts. Peter and Paul**. Behind the church and the city hall are the remains of the Roman fort. On the mountain above the city is the **Church of St. Apollinaris** (1839 – 42). A Benedictine abbey was built on this site during the 12th century. The mortal remains of St. Apollinaris have rested here since 1530. Not far from the city are the **piers of the former railway bridge**. The Americans succeeded in crossing the Rhine here when the German Army failed to blow up the bridge in 1945. Today, the "Peace Museum" **(Friedensmuseum)** located within the towers commemorates the events.

Remagen, Bridge towers

Unkel, Rhine Panorama

## Unkel

At the base of the Leidenberg lies the wine town of Unkel. The famous **"Unkeler Funkeler"** wine can be tasted in the many wine bars. Visitors can see picturesque half-timbered buildings, the **remains of the old city wall** and the early **Gothic parish church**. In the **Freiligrath House** (built in 1760) lived the poet Ferdinand Freiligrath (1810 – 1876). The author Stefan Andres (1906 – 1970) lived in Unkel from 1950 until 1961. In addition to hiking in the **Rhine-Westerwald Wildlife Park**, a side-trip to **Vilszelt Castle** in the part of the city called Heister is also worthwhile. The water-surrounded castle from the 11th century was restored in the 18th century.

## Bad Honnef

Bad Honnef is situated at the foot of the Siebengebirge mountains. The little town has been famous as a spa since the turn of the century. The **medicinal springs** make drinking and bathing cures possible. Spa guests can find rest and relaxation in the modern **spa house**, surrounded by the magnificently landscaped spa garden. In the center of Bad Honnef, lovingly restored old half-timbered buildings and buildings from the classical period and the late 19th century invite a stroll through the town. At the market is the late Gothic **Catholic parish church of St. John the Baptist**. Inside is a sacristy dating from 1500. Well-preserved half-timbered buildings are also found in the surrounding quarters of the city. The ruins of Löwenburg Castle from the 12th and 13th centuries can be visited on the **Löwenberg** northeast of town. A footpath leads over a bridge to **Grafenwerth Island**.

# Rolandsbogen

A high window arch, all that is left of a twelfth century castle at Rolands-eck, is not only surrounded by thick ivy growth, but by sayings as well. As legend would have it, the Knight Roland, one of Charlemagne's warriors, was caught gazing with longing through the huge window toward Nonnenwerth Island. Upon this, his brokenhearted bride ran away to live out the rest of her days in a convent.

Roland's Arch (Rolandsbogen)

Nonnenwerth Island

## Nonnenwerth Island

The Benedictine order founded a monastery on this island in the Rhine in 1122. The composer Franz Liszt lived here in 1840 – 41. A grammar school (Gymnasium) for girls and boys is associated with the present day Franciscan cloister.

## Rhöndorf

The first Federal Chancellor of the Federal Republic of Germany, Dr. Konrad Adenauer, lived in the small town of Rhöndorf. Today the house and the terraced rose garden are home to an exhibition about his life.

Rhöndorf

## Drachenfels

In 1147, the Archbishops of Cologne built **Drachenfels** Castle high above Königswinter opposite Rolandseck Castle in order to make it easier to enforce collection of tariffs on the Rhine by establishing a military stronghold on the right bank of the river as well. Beginning in 1402, the sovereign territory of Electoral Cologne's Little Land of Drachenfels ("Drachenfelser Ländchen") extended all the way to the slope of the northern Eifel Mountains. The destruction of Drachenfels Castle high above Königswinter was the work of troops from Cologne: the imposing fortress was demolished in 1634, in the midst of the Thirty Years' War, in order to keep it from falling into the hands of the advancing Swedes. Since then, the castle has lain in ruins, of which much of the castle precincts can still be seen. In the 19th and 20th centuries, the castle had to be prevented more than once from collapsing into a stone quarry from which the basalt glass used in constructing Cologne Cathedral was quarried. According to legend, young Siegfried is supposed to have conquered the dragon on the "Dragon Rock" (Drachenfels). The "Dragon's Cave" **(Drachenhöhle)** and the Hall of the Nibelungs **(Nibelungenhalle)** can be seen on the way to Drachenfels.

Drachenfels and Drachenfels-Restaurant

Drachenburg Palace

## Drachenburg Palace

Halfway up the hill toward the ruins of Drachenfels castle, W. Hoffmann built a magnificent palace on a commission from Stephan Sarter from 1879 until 1884. The native of Bonn had the palace built because he wanted to compete with the Bavarian King Ludwig II, who had several royal residences built in Bavaria at the same time. For this reason, Drachenburg Palace's angles and towers bear an external resemblance to Neuschwanstein. Because it is relatively new, Drachenburg Palace really does not belong to the chain of castles in the Siebengebirge Mountains range. The imitation was far more authentic, however, than many 19th century restorations of the real thing. The palace can be reached by a **cog railway**, which began operation in 1883, by a steep footpath or by donkey. There is a **wildlife park** all around the castle in which local wildlife in open surroundings is very popular with visitors of all ages.

## Königswinter

Charmingly situated at the base of the Drachenfels in the **Sieben-gebirge mountain** range lies the climatic health resort and excursion destination of Königswinter. The town's quiet little alleys, lined with picturesque half-timbered houses, invite visitors to go for a stroll. The **Catholic parish church of St. Remigius** was built in 1779 on the site of a Romanesque church. In the interior, the high altar, parts of the baroque chancel and parts of the organ from the time when the church was constructed are preserved. In the church there is an arm reliquary of St. Margaretha (14th century). From the promenade on the banks of Rhine, one has a lovely view of Mehlem and the Rod-derberg. Culture lovers will find what they are looking for in the his-torical **Siebengebirgs-Museum** or in the **Hall of the Nibelungs** at the foot of the Drachenfels. There is also a **reptile zoo** here. Cistercian monks from nearby **Heisterbach Monastery** laid the foundation for the town's winemaking tradition many years ago. "Dragon's Blood"

Königswinter, Half-timbered houses

Locomobile

89

Königswinter

**(Drachenblut)** is the name of the well-known red wine that grows in the area southwest of Königswinter and which can be tasted in many cosy wine bars.

## Petersberg

Guests of state are not the only ones welcome on the Petersberg. The one-time hotel served as the headquarters for the High Commissioners of the Western Allies following World War II. Later it was converted into a luxury hotel for heads of state. Now, after further renovation, the building complex serves the German Federal Government as a guest house. The "Restaurant Steigenberger" is open to the general public.

Petersberg

Bonn-Bad Godesberg, Kurhaus „Redoute"

## Bonn-Bad Godesberg

Toward the end of the 13th century the last Elector of Cologne founded the **mineral spa** Godesberg, which is located on the Rhine River.
**The fortress Godesburg** was built in 1210 on a basalt peak above
the city on a site which was used for ritual sacrifices in pre-Roman
times. This fortress was demolished more than 350 years later during a siege. Only the outer walls and somewhat remote castle precincts remain. On the northern face of the castle hill is the Baroque
**Chapel of St. Michael**, built 1697 – 1699. The spa district in the town
is just right for a stroll. The focus is on the classical spa house **"Redoute"**, built 1790 – 1792, it hosted state receptions into the 90's. In
the "drinking pavilion" (Trinkpavillion) bubbles the "New Electoral
Spring" **(Neue Kurfürstenquelle)**. The Electoral Bath (1964) and the
**Theatre** (1986) and **Chamber Theatre** were erected between the
parks. Until the relocation of parliament and parts of the German
Government during 1998/99, Bad Godesberg was a favorite duty station and dwelling place of civil servants and diplomats from Bonn.
Bad Godesberg was annexed to the City of Bonn in 1969.

Bonn-Bad Godesberg, Godesburg

Bonn, Market and City Hall

Beethoven Memorial

## Bonn

Since 1949, Bonn has become known the world over: after World War II, the university town on the Rhine became the capital of the Federal Republic of Germany. The Romans founded the "Castra Bonnensia" as one of the first of their fortresses more than 2,000 years ago. Bonn was the residence of the Archbishops of Cologne from 1238 until 1794. The famous modern **university** was constructed 1697 – 1725 by Enrico Zuccali and Robert de Cotte as an electoral palace. The residence was converted into an institution of higher education in 1818. The group of buildings includes the **Coblence Gate**. The **Baroque City Hall** (1737/38) is in the heart of the old city. The **birthplace of composer Ludwig van Beethoven** (1770 – 1827) is at Bonngasse 20. According to legend, Saint Helena was the founder of a small collegiate church, on the foundations of which the five-towered minster was erected in the 11th through the 13th centuries. The old building also includes a partially preserved crypt. To the south, the building joins on to a two story cloister (12th century). The government quarters located in the southern part of town lost some of its prominence due to the relocation of parts of the German Government to Berlin in 1998/99. Six federal ministries have their first duty stations, and two their secondary duty stations, in the "Federal City". The "Lange Eugen", the former House of Representatives, houses the center of the UN-Campus established in 2006.

University

Bonn

## Cologne

Even the Romans recognized the advantages of the position on the Rhine and founded a "Colonia" here ca. 50 AD which was named after Agrippina, who was the wife of Kaiser Claudius and was born in Germania. Cologne belonged to the Franconian kingdom since the end of the fifth century. Charlemagne elevated the city to the status of an archbishopric. Alongside Lübeck, the city was at times one of

Cologne Cathedral

the most important bases of the Hanseatic League during the Middle Ages. Cologne was taken over by the Prussians together with the Rhine province. Much of city was destroyed in World War II. The landmark of the city is the massive **Cologne Cathedral**, a masterwork of the High Gothic period and one of the largest cathedrals in Europe. Construction began in 1248 and was not completed until 1880. The relics of the Magi are kept in the golden Magi shrine **(Dreikönigenschrein)** above the high altar. The famous picture "Homage of the Kings" by Stephan Lochner is located in the choir aisle. The early Gothic statuary, crosses, glass windows and the treasurevault are also remarkable. The towers are 157 meter (nearly 515 feet) high and a climb up the more than 500 steps to the top of the south tower is rewarded by a magnificent panoramic view over the rooftops of the city all the way to the Siebengebirge Mountains. Today the Cathedral is the residence of the Archbishop of Cologne and thus the center of the largest diocese in Germany. There are also important art treasures to be found in the **twelve Romanesque churches**. From the Cathedral one comes directly on to the "High Street" **(Hohe Straße)**, where the shopping district begins. Visitors can find the famous original cologne or **"Kölnisch Wasser"** in the Glockengasse, house number 4711. A carillon plays in

Cologne, Old Market with City Hall Tower and Monument Jan von Werth

Hahnentor Gate

the building with the neo-Gothic facade. Another attraction is the old city on the Rhine, in which the bars serve Kölsch, a top-fermented, light beer, on tap. The **old city hall** was built in the 15th and 16th centuries on the ruins of the Roman Praetorium. The city's "front parlor", the **Gürzenich Festival Hall**, is also nearby. It was erected between 1437 and 1444 as a commercial and festival building. The historic heart of the city is surrounded by the remnants of the medieval **city wall** and its three portals. Just in back of the Cathedral is the **Roman-Germanic Museum**, which was erected over the Roman mosaic of Dionysus. The **Wallraff-Richartz Museum** and the **Museum Ludwig** house important works of art by renowned painters. Today, Cologne is an important transportation hub in Central Europe. In addition to ten superhighways which lead to and from the city in a star formation, Cologne has a large main train station, a river port, eight bridges across the Rhine and the Cologne-Bonn Airport. Large commercial and industrial companies are headquartered in the Cathedral city. The fools are loose every year in January and February during **Cologne's world-famous Carnival**.

△ Cologne Cathedral and St. Martin's Church    ▽ Cologne Cathedral, Interior View

96

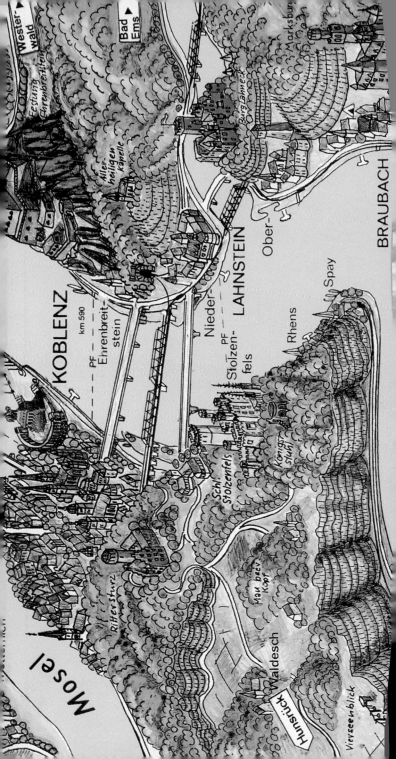

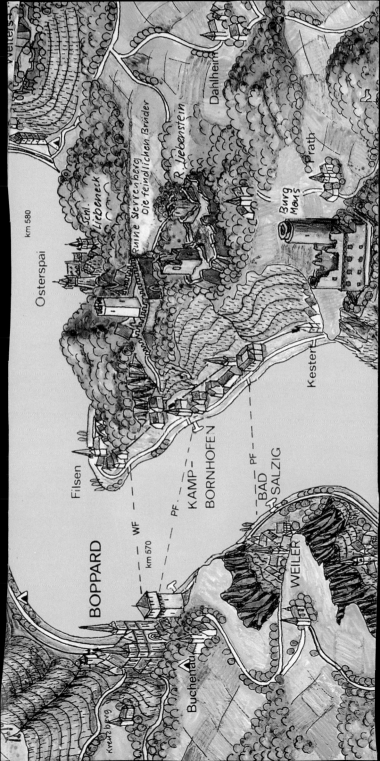

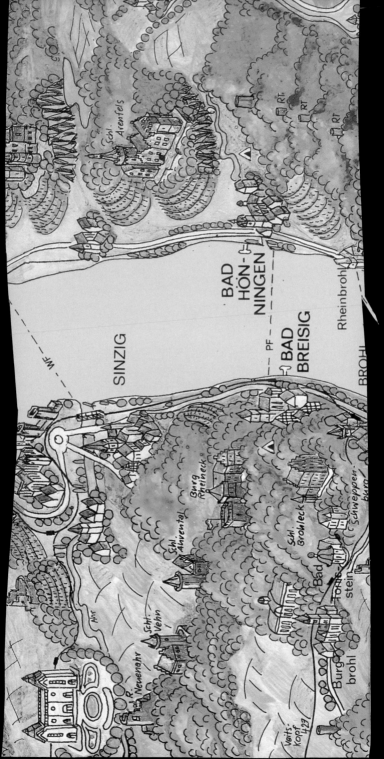

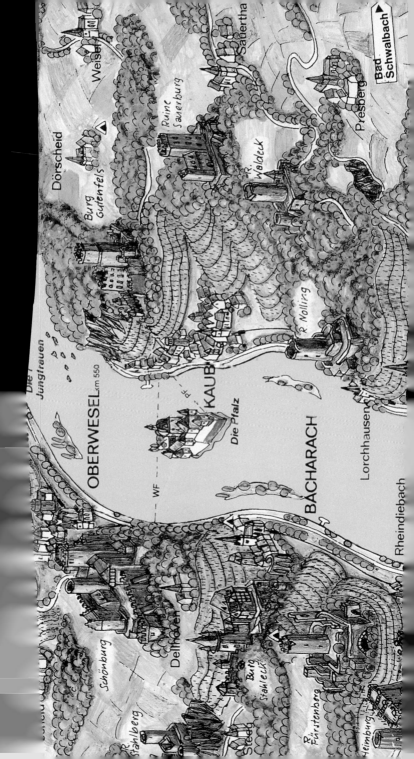

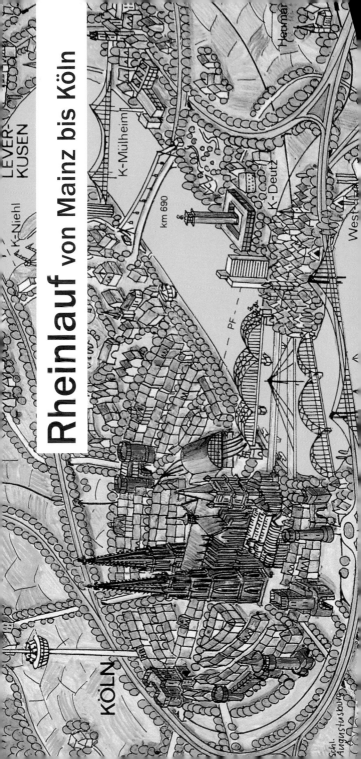

WIESBADEN

M-Kastel

Kostheim

Biebrich

W-Biebrich

Rettbergs-Aue

Budenheim

Peters-Aue

PF

km 500

Main

MAINZ

INGELHEIM

B. Kreuznach

Marien-born

Finthen

Die im Strom eingezeichneten Zahlen entsprechen der fortlaufenden Kilometrierung des Rheins und sind in großen Zahlen an den Rheinufern abzulesen.

PF – Personenfähre    AF – Autofähre

rahmelverlag®

deutschlandkultur. entdecken!

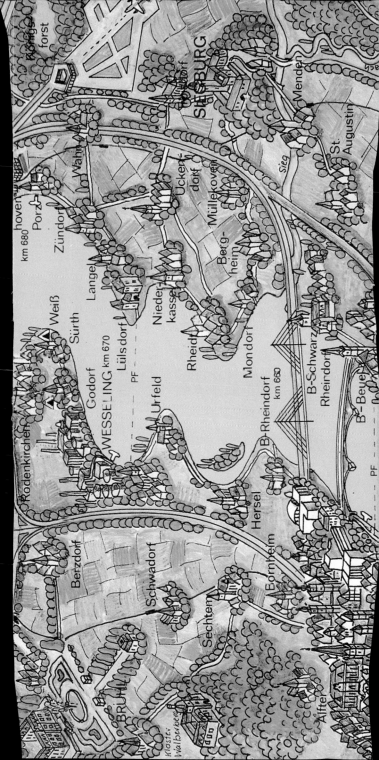

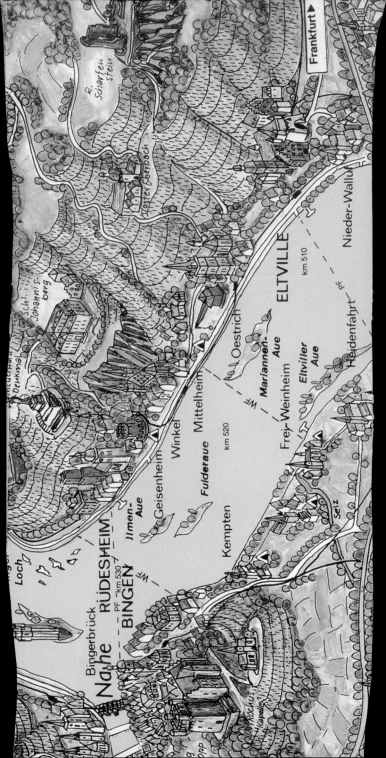

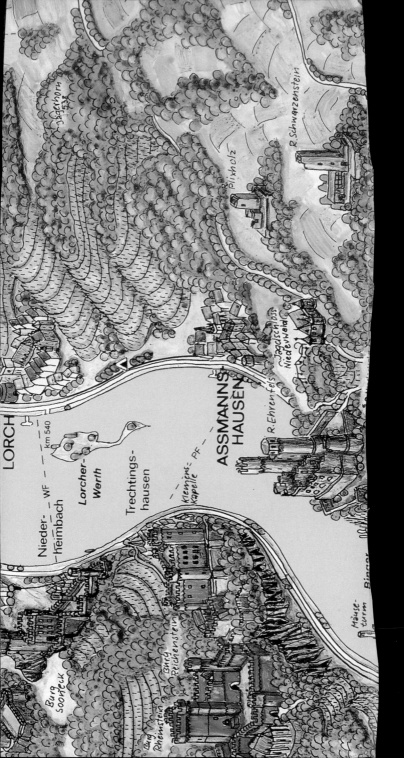

Jägerhorn 538

R. Schwarzenstein

Plixholz

R. Ehrenfels

Jagdschloss Niederwald

LORCH

km 540

Nieder- — WF — Heimbach

Lorcher- Werth

Trechtings- hausen

Klemens- Kapelle PF.

ASSMANNS- HAUSEN

Burg Soonbeck

Burg Rheinstein

Burg Reichenstein

Mäuse- turm

Binger